MW01180856

ISBN 9798689742540

Missouri Baptist Foundation
PO Box 1113
Jefferson CIty, MO 65102-1113

www.myfinacialpastor.com
www.mbfn.org

table of contents

THE AUTHOR
DR. NEIL FRANKS

Dr. Neil Franks is the President and Treasurer of the Missouri Baptist Foundation. Dr. Franks has pastored churches of all sizes; most recently spending the last decade leading First Baptist Church in Branson, Missouri. The church more than doubled their budget and nearly tripled in attendance under his leadership.

Dr. Franks served as President of the Missouri Baptist Convention in 2014 and 2015, and Vice President of the SBC Pastors' Conference in 2016. He has also served on the Board of Trustees for Southwest Baptist University.

A native of Malvern, Arkansas, Dr. Franks earned a Bachelor of Arts Degree in Speech Communications from Henderson State University, Arkadelphia, Arkansas. He holds a Master of Divinity from Southwestern Baptist Theological Seminary, Ft. Worth, Texas and a Doctor of Ministry from Midwestern Baptist Theological Seminary, Kansas City, Missouri.

INTRODUCTION

I write this book as a long-time pastor. During those years, I saw our Lord do incredible things both spiritually and financially.

Our weekly attendance tripled, and our annual budget more than doubled. We built a $2.7 million community center and paid it off in less than three years.

Not only did we expand ministry, but we finished in the black every year while seeing almost double-digit budget growth annually, all while increasing our missions giving by three-fold.

Most people have an idea about the way they desire for things to work out. Part of my role as a pastor, is to warn people about what is ahead. The path you are on, not your intended one, determines your ultimate destination.

What you decide has the potential to cause significant harm to your family after you are gone and prevent them from experiencing all of God's blessings.

Think about it.

No author calls you to be like everybody else. Many books call you to something higher, more worthy of your significant skills and pursuits.

This book is similar in some respects, only I want to call you to a new level of Christian living which is lacking in the church today.

A place where the Jesus follower no longer views his money as his own, but rather a gift from God.

I want you to experience the joy of serving the Lord by building a financial plan whose purpose is to utilize the wealth the Lord has granted you to advance the cause of Christ.

Instead of starting this story at the beginning, lets start at the end.

The greatest opportunity to give financially may come long after you are gone. You won't have any expenses, cars, or kids. Your resources can still make an impact in the lives of others.

I can understand fears, but why are Christians not leaving significant portions of their estates to support the ministries they love after they die? Especially since their earthly wealth has continued to increase? We have started spending more money on ourselves than on the things of God.

A 2020 survey found only 32% of Americans have a will. If you are part of the 68% who do not have plans in place or the 32% who do, join me on this journey to better financial preparation.

I want you to see an estate plan as a way to experience the joy of giving on a grand scale. There is something deeply satisfying about supporting ministries where you personally see and feel God's presence.

Jesus has called us to be stewards of our finances just like the widow and her two mites. Our money is not our own, it is a gift from the Lord.

Instead of asking you to give large amounts of money now, I want you to consider creating an estate plan that will continue to advance the Gospel long after you are gone. Consider how we are going to fund Gospel ministry over the next twenty years.

We are in a dual crisis of the most massive transfer of wealth in human history, taking place at the same time we are experiencing the most significant decline in the sheer number of Evangelicals.

We are failing to convince the next generation to support the work of established institutional ministries, at precisely the time we are losing a generation who did.

Are any of these things inherently wrong or unBibilical? No, but it is important we prepare for the future.

As a long time pastor and now the president of the Missouri Baptist Foundation, I feel I can present a unique perspective on finances. My purpose is to encourage Jesus followers to leverage their wealth and finances by:

GETTING WELL   LIVING WELL

Sincerely,

Neil Franks

FINISHING WELL

Dr. Neil Franks CEP®
Your Financial Pastor

CHAPTER ONE

ESTATE PLANNING

Our goal is straightforward.

In less than 45 minutes, we want you to move from thinking about an estate plan to actually creating one. This plan may not be perfect, but rather one you can improve upon and feel secure about.

A completed plan can take care of your loved ones by passing your assets in the most cost and time-efficient manner possible. It can also make provisions for your own self-care, should you become unable to act on your own. Most importantly, it also gives you the opportunity to be generous toward God and further His Kingdom long after you are gone.

Let us begin by overcoming the word "estate." Most people do not think of what they own (their assets) as an "estate." When I use the word "estate" many people assume it does not apply to them.

And so, they avoid it just like the old joke about someone who was not too bright; "When the Lord was passing out brains, the person thought God said "trains" and they got out of the way." When I say estate plan, do not get out of the way, rather use your brain to jump on the train.

An "estate" is just another way of saying "assets" or something you own. Even if you only own part of the asset, and the bank owns the rest; it still belongs to you. When you die, somebody will take possession of it. Estate planning is the process of creating the pathway of that transfer in the way you want.

So, in other words, an estate plan is a plan for where your assets (the things you own) will go, if something were to happen to you.

Now, I know what some of you are thinking,

"WELL, I DON'T CARE, I WON'T BE AROUND ANYMORE."

Which while accurate, is pretty short-sighted because the people you love will still be around and what happens to them should be of utmost importance to *you*.

I remember shaming a group of men on Father's Day, telling them if they were "real men" who <u>really</u> loved their wife and children, they would have enough life insurance to adequately provide for her and the children, should something ever happened to them.

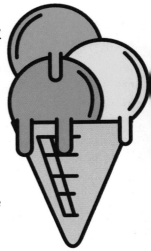

There were more than a few stunned faces in the congregation that morning.

It's ok, because I passed out coupons for Cold Stone Ice Cream for them to soak their bruised egos in with their family afterward.

I know, life insurance may sound like a strange topic for a Sunday morning sermon but taking care of those you love is a very Biblical concept.

Consider I Timothy 5:8, "But if anyone does not provide for his relatives, and especially for members of his household, he has denied the faith and is worse than an unbeliever."

Now I am not here to tell you "exactly how" you are to provide for your family, particularly after you have passed from this life to the next as that is up to the individual believer and their circumstances. However, not making "any" provision for them is _UnBiblical_.

Since you are reading this book, I commend you for taking the first step. Planning requires time, effort, and a little bit of money to legally get all of the paperwork in order. But it will be worth your effort and your family will thank you.

There is another group of you who say,

"WELL, I DON'T REALLY HAVE ANYTHING OF VALUE; THE EFFORT WILL NOT BE WORTH MY TIME."

It is true that some of us have more than others, but you are responsible for what you do have.

Do you remember the story Jesus told of the talents? One servant received five; the other received two, and the other received just one. Jesus did not expect the one who had two talents to return five; he judged them on what they did with the talents they had. You will not be accountable to God for what He never gave you, but you can be pretty sure you will have some explaining to do for what he did give you.

If you think about it, in some ways, the less you have of something, the more precious it is. Isn't that why gold is more valuable than sandstone? I mean, if Bill Gates drops a $20 bill, he may not even stop to pick it up; while you and I would think differently.

The same is true for those who do not think they have much. Now, obviously, you do not want to spend $5,000 on an estate plan when you only have a few dollars and a small family. However, crafting a plan is still helpful, and prevents the burden from falling to others.

A third group of people are thinking something else, (You may be one of them.)

"I WILL JUST LET MY KIDS SORT IT OUT AFTER I AM GONE."

That may be tempting if your children are adults and get along, but you are forgetting something important; your estate involves more than just your children. Consider the outcome of not making a plan; you may end up costing your children time and money as they sort things out. Instead of easy access to your estate, they may be prohibited by law from taking any action for months or even years.

Without proof of legal empowerment, heirs are not always able to act. In many cases, even if they are, it may be only be after the case has appeared in front of a judge. During the days in court, your family's time and money will be wasted.

In addition to the legal issues, delays, and costs, one might also want to consider the relational stress forced upon the heirs.

As a pastor, I have had more than one uncomfortable situation with a divided family.

Everyone got along without a hitch while mom and/or dad were alive, but now that money is at stake; well, let's just say not everyone allows their good side to show.

However, the greatest loss caused by life without an estate plan may be the lack of control in how you want your assets distributed. The government does not understand your family dynamics.

- Does one child just blow through money like the government?

- Does one sibling get pushed around by the others?

- Is there a grandchild with a special need?

- Are you concerned about substance abuse running in the family?

These real-life instances, along with a long list of others, should challenge any person who assumes the family will work it out.

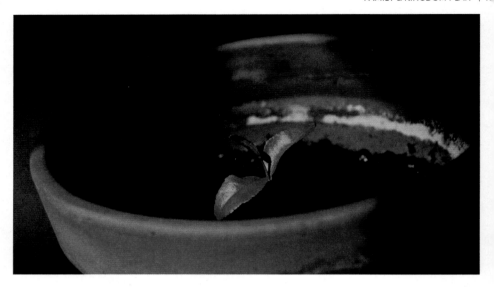

Having an estate plan is vital for success of any kind, but especially in your family's future.

Hopefully I have convinced you to do something with estate planning. If so, where do we start? Well, we start at the very beginning, at least that is what Julie Andrews (I mean Marie Von Trapp) would do.

Let us build a Biblical foundation for our planning of the future. We could start in the Garden of Eden, but I am going to skip over the Genesis part of the story, and the "a man should leave his father and mother part."

Instead, I am going to pick up in the middle of a story where we find a son who is left unprepared to manage his father's significant inheritance which results in destruction.

If you are not so much interested in what the Bible says, or you don't need any more convincing about what is at stake, or are just ready to jump into the estate planning process, you can skip Chapter 2 and join me in Chapter 3.

For everyone else, join me in Chapter 2 of Estate Planning to meet the world's loneliest man.

CHAPTER TWO

REHOBOAM

He stood there all alone.

The kind of alone you only feel when you are in the middle of a crowd of people. A bunch of ear whisperers each offering advice counter to the previous. Opposite even.

The warm breath barely recedes and the natural coolness of the sensitive ear canal returns before the next guidance giver can warm it once again.

The physical response of which was much more comforting than the intellectual dissonance of not knowing to whom should he listen?

He would have to make a decision, and make it soon, if not for the kingdom but his own sake.

It had only been a few hours since he had inherited his father's kingdom. But already people were in his ear. His father had built a massive empire, a world power, and a lavish lifestyle. Yes, the foundation had begun to crack under the strain, but it was holding, at least for now.

Enter into Rehoboam's world. His father, Solomon, had just died. While many were sad, others saw an opportunity.

Over time Solomon had begun to raise taxes, conscript workers, make allegiances he could not keep, and oppressed those around him to keep it all going. For many, his death was a relief.

There was hope that the 41-year-old son of Solomon would make better decisions. At least that is what his father's advisors had hoped —especially those from the Northern Kingdom.

There had always been tension among the tribes. They were, in fact, a bunch of brothers, but David had brought them together and held them together, Solomon had expanded their influence but at a high cost.

Now it was Rehoboam's job, one he was not prepared to take. He wasn't sure to whom to listen, he made a beginner's mistake, he listened to the wrong people.

I cannot imagine the pressure placed on a spouse who lost their partner. I have only known the loss of a parent, but even that loss clouded my vision for months.

I have always counseled the remaining spouse to put off decision making for at least six months, but I am not sure even that is enough time.

I think of what a friend of mine is going through right now; her husband, the pastor of a large church, just died in a one-car accident, leaving her behind to raise three boys. How her world must be spinning, and so too the world of the people you leave behind.

MAYBE NOT AS DRAMATICALLY, BUT JUST AS PROFOUNDLY.

She, like your loved ones, will be surrounded by people, many with good intentions offering advice. Buy this annuity, pay off your house, move to Florida...the list will go on, and your loved one will be there in the center feeling all alone.

It is for that reason you are building an estate plan. To provide help and guidance and a plan, not to rule their life forever, but for a season.

To provide a way forward, to protect those who offer unwarranted advice. Your careful planning and effort now will provide the comfort and presence of your love.

But not for Rehoboam. His father's advisors surrounded him and told him to lighten up on the people. Change a few policies, lower the taxes, show some heart.

His personal advisors, the buddy's he grew up with, told him the opposite, to lay it on thick. Teach the people a lesson, let them know your dad was tough, but you are tougher. Your little finger is thicker than your father's waist. You must show them.

And at that moment, Rehoboam proved he was not comparable to his father at all. His father adept at negotiation and getting "buy-in" from those around him. A man gifted in the "art" of the deal, Rehoboam, unskilled, bewildered, unprepared, makes a poor decision, one for which he had not trained.

All his father had built, built on what David his grandfather established, all fell apart because Rehoboam was not ready.

Because Rehoboam listened to his buddies and refused the counsel of his father's advisors and rejected the northern tribes' requests. Those tribes, ten of the twelve, turned to an alternative leader Jeroboam.

A trusted lieutenant of his father's, a more skilled leader who had tried to lead a rebellion earlier and had been sent away to Egypt, united them and became the leader of the new nation of Israel. Never again would the kingdom be united.

In two hundred years, the northern tribes would be destroyed by Assyria, in another hundred years, the southern tribes by the Babylonians. It would be almost 2500 years before the Jewish people would be free again.

Now, I don't mean to imply that your failure to provide an estate plan will have national ramifications for two-plus millennia. However, how well you prepare your loved ones for your passing, will have a lasting effect.

Remember, they will be missing you, resulting in emotional distress. Others will be filling their ears with all sorts of advice, and they will feel alone.

But imagine, instead in that moment, they can turn to a plan. A plan you conceived for them out of love, so they won't have to be all alone.

Your estate plan will be a trusted resource where you have already laid out the steps for them to take to get through those crucial first months. They will feel your love and care for them, and their steps will be steady because they will know they are not alone.

Let's get started, by asking the first of <u>six questions.</u>

CHAPTER THREE

WHAT DO YOU HAVE?

The first step in building an estate plan is understanding the depth and breadth of your own estate.

Remembering that an estate is really the entirety of your assets, the total of things that you own. Items can be either fully or partially owned, or even if you have an interest toward ownership. It is best to identify them all out in detail. There are lots of ways to do this. You can simply start with a piece of paper and make lists.

Identify any bank accounts, followed by real estate, retirement accounts, vehicles, collections, personal property, insurance, and/or investment accounts. You are recording any item of value, whether tangible or intangible, physically in your presence or somewhere far off, the goal is to get it all recorded.

We at the <u>MBF</u>, have a guide you can <u>download</u> from our website, or request to be emailed to you to assist with the process.

You can even search to come up with a variety of other resources or guides online. Some of these can be fillable PDF's (digital forms that you can complete and store on your computer for safekeeping.) The form does not matter, it is the planning that makes the difference.

I can hear the push-back already. "I don't have anything of value," you say. Well, we recently had a client who was thinking the same thing. They had never married and had no children and decided he wanted all of his estate to benefit a Gospel advancing ministry, but he said he did not really have anything.

So, one of our team members went over to his "house." Which is first off an indication of wealth, he owned a house. Not a mansion by any means, but still an average home in an average neighborhood and it will serve as the centerpiece of his estate planning.

There was a car in the garage, another asset of some value, but other than that, he insisted, he had nothing else of value.

Until on the tour of the nothingness he led us downstairs to the basement.

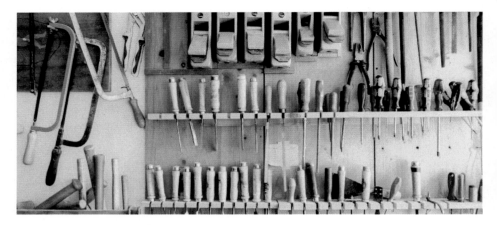

And there was the man's woodworking shop. In addition to the heavy and expensive equipment was a wall full of "bits." You know the kind that shapes the wood into, well, different shapes. "How much does that one cost?" asked our staff member. "Well that one is $25, and that one over there $50, and that one $75." After a few minutes of such an exercise, the man confessed, "I guess I may have more than I thought."

Just like the old song reminds us, count your blessings, name them one by one, and it might just surprise you what the Lord has done. You might be surprised by what you actually have come into possession. So let's start with the obvious.

Property

Do you own a house, mobile home, condo, or some land? Write that down. Go ahead and put addresses down as well.

Do you have a timeshare someplace or lake property? Are you anticipating inheriting some land from a family member? Put those down as it will be helpful later.

Bank Accounts

Do you have a checking account, savings account and/or money market account? List those in another column, including at least part of the account number and the bank name or location.

What about CD's? Although they are not really an account, they are often at the same location as the others. Do you have a safe deposit box? Where is the key?

Retirement Accounts

Do you have employer-sponsored retirement?

Do you have IRA's whether traditional or Roth?

Do you have a government or military benefit?

All current beneficiary information needs to be listed.

Investment Accounts

Do you own stocks and bonds?

Or other financial positions in market traded accounts?

Business Interest

Do you own a business?

What is the arrangement? Who are the other business partners?

Life Insurance

Personal Property

Do you have life insurance policies, with whom, at what amounts?

Cars, motorcycles, RV's boats, guns, or art collections or any collections for that matter in your possession?

Disability plans, burial policies, and the like in your possession?

Furniture or other furnishings?

Have you taken out any such policies on other people, that maybe they are not aware of it?

Anything of significant value: memorabilia, computers, farm equipment, tractors, or clothing of unusual worth?

The beneficiary names should be up to date and cataloged.

All of these should be listed.

Children

Another kind of an asset, your most valuable.

What are the names and ages? Do they have special needs?

Passwords & Processes

This is a newer category of asset as our passwords guard much of our financial lives.

Does your spouse or someone know these passwords and for what they are used?

Even more important, what about the processes you use to pay for things? How do you make a deposit or a debit on the kid's college savings fund?

Anything you can think of, list it on the page.

Then there is the other side of things. If you took a business class in college, you might remember the asset side has a liability side as well.

Debts

A proper listing of mortgages, obligations, and other encumbrances would need to be listed as well since the requirements on most of those will pass on the next generation.

Debt does not magically disappear at one's passing.

Making a list of assets is often the most challenging step, but it is an important one.

Without it, you will not be able to create your plan appropriately.

HOW DID YOU DO?

Did you come up with more than you thought you might?

Did you consult with your spouse? Now is not the time to be hiding things from one another; it is the time to work together to create a comprehensive list.

The lists will always be changing as you make purchases and get rid of things. You may inherit something as well.

It is ok to have an incomplete list, but it does need an annual review.

Let's take what you have so far and move on to the next step in our process by answering the next question.

CHAPTER FOUR

WHERE DO YOU WANT IT TO GO?

Once you have completed your inventory in the <u>Family and Kingdom Workbook</u>.

Where do you want it to go?

Who or Whom? I never really know which one is right, do you want to have what? You need to include a proper destination for every item on your list.

The technical term is a beneficiary- one who derives advantage from something.

The beneficiary receives the "benefit," in this case, of the asset being handed down to them upon your passing.

So the next step is to determine who is going to receive what. In many instances, it will be your spouse. If that is the case, it is pretty simple; everything goes to them.

Hopefully, your spouse will feel the same way, and the documents will be mirrors of one another, creating reciprocity between the two of you.

It is in the second stage of decision making, the naming of beneficiaries where it can become a bit more interesting and time-consuming. (You will want to make sure that your spouse's name appears as the beneficiary wherever possible on any titled assets, we will get to more of that later.)

Afterward, then you would list children as the next beneficiaries of the estate. In other words upon the second death of the two of you, your children will inherit in equal shares your estate.

That, of course, is in a perfect scenario. But this world is not perfect, and your children probably aren't either.

Maybe one of them needs the money more, or one of them can't handle money very well, or struggles with substance abuse, or is in the midst of a less than pretty divorce. Maybe you have a blended family yourself, and you don't want his/her kids inheriting the farm that has been in your family a hundred years.

Am I exhausting you yet? I, too, am an avoider. So when I have these decisions to make, I tend to believe whatever lie I make up so I won't have to make them.

Our previously identified lie, "Won't it all just all work out," seems to be coming back up. It won't just all work out, this needs your attention to provide guidance or it will only be a bigger mess.

So let's look closely at naming beneficiaries.

One easy way to approach asset distribution is strictly from a percentage basis. If you have two kids, everything is divided into two equal half shares, with each child receiving half. Three shares with three kids or 33% each or 25% if you had four kids. Pretty simple.

This approach; however, will require a determination of value(s) either through liquidation or via appraisals as it can get a little more complicated and expensive.

Let's say the most valuable item is the family farm. A 200-acre parcel and you have four kids. Pretty easy arithmetic, each of them get 50 acres. But one child needs the cash and wants to sell his portion, but the other three want him to keep it in the family, but the other three do not have the funds to "buy" him out.

All of a sudden, a blessing can become a burden.

Another way to make distributions is to do it on an item by item basis. This strategy is often helpful in those "non-cash valuable" but "sentimental" ones.

In my family, there is a nativity scene my deceased mother made with her own hands while taking a class as an army wife. I can assure you it has no "auction estimated" value, but I anticipate it will be the only thing my brother and I may fight about when my father passes.

It will be a shame for the wise men and angels to live in Arkansas while baby Jesus and the shepherds live in Missouri, but I am not currently seeing another solution.

This methodology can also be utilized with other items in the estate. One child may get the farm in the country, the other the house on the beach, and the third inherit the Swiss Chalet.

Ok, so that may not directly apply to your estate, and it may be more like Bob gets the 1974 Pinto, Jane gets the Camry with 273,000 miles, and Tina gets the Chevy truck with three tires, but with the new mudflaps bought for Christmas last year.

It will be up to you to determine the general values, and who you want to get what, if you don't just do a percentage methodology.

It will be up to you, but you must have this written down, and wherever possible in one of the legal documents we are going to mention later on.

Some families even sit down and share in person the plan, so there will be no surprises after the funeral. Just make sure that if you make any changes to the documents, you have the same conversations. The dissonance between the verbal and the legal is where family splitting trouble resides.

But here is also where you can think about your estate benefiting more than just one generation as it dawns on you; it does not all have to be distributed at once.

You can leave something for the grandchildren. Maybe you want to leave something to create an education fund that would allow the grandchildren to have a portion or all of their schooling paid by building an education endowment. You could leave a specific portion of the estate to be invested with the growth to offset the cost of education.

Maybe you have a person in the family with a particular need. Say a developmental or learning need where you want to ensure their care. (Special legal arrangements generally referred to as a special needs trust can be created with the help of legal counsel to provide maximum benefit without risking current or anticipated governmental benefits).

Maybe you have a special friend who has an appreciation for a specific item of yours in which your children have no interest.

Or, someone you know has been unusually kind, and you wish to return the favor. It is at this stage that you think and pray for God's guidance on how you can be a blessing.

I also need to remind you that once you make it to heaven, you won't need your stuff. They don't take the US dollar in heaven. Neither do they in that other eternal destination (in case that is your back-up plan.)

You could use a portion of your estate, maybe even a significant portion, to help other people find heaven as well. Take the opportunity of your estate plan to leave a gift at your passing to the ministries you support during your lifetime.

Some people will leave a specific portion of their estate to their church, many choosing to leave 10% going to their local congregation. Others will include all of their ministry and other philanthropic giving in their plan by creating an additional heir.

If you have two children, instead of dividing everything by two, they consider all of their other giving as a third child and divide the entire estate into thirds.

Still, other people decide to take a more extended approach to their estate planning. Instead of seeking immediate distribution of their assets, they, through long-term investing, aim to double the value of their estate and give it away twice. Once to charity and once to family.

I will talk more about this in a later chapter. Your task, for now, is to take all that you have and determine "who" you want to get "what."

It may sound daunting at first, and maybe a little morbid, but once you get started, it actually can get kind of fun. It is like Christmas shopping, but without all of the picking stuff out, you just hand out the things you already have after you no longer need it!

Join us in chapter 5 to figure out how to get it all distributed.

CHAPTER FIVE

HOW DO YOU WANT IT TO GET THERE?

Back in the day when I was growing up, there was a series of television commercials that featured Fram oil filters. The kind mechanic explained how he was repairing the newer four-cylinder engines more often than, the larger ones. They were working harder, much harder, than the other motors because they were smaller.

In the commercial behind the "nice" auto mechanic was another mechanic who was working on one of those small engines. The sage in the back would affirm certain statements the mechanic in the front made. Like how replacing your oil filter was relatively inexpensive compared to paying a guy like him in the back to repair your small hard-working engine. A fate you could avoid by installing one of those Fram oil filters.

The whole, unpretentious commercial ended by the "nice" mechanic holding up the invoice and saying, so you can pay me now or pay him later.

We face something similar in our conversation in this chapter as we move to the next question in our estate planning. After we have identified "what" we have and "who" we want to get it, we now ask the question, "How do we want it to get there?" And there are only two options.

The first way is slowly, publicly, and with a high expense; where attorneys and the courts get a cut of the estate first.

The other way is quickly, privately, with lower cost and most of the estate preserved for the beneficiary.

If you want the first way, then you do nothing. Just like in the Fram commercial, keep doing nothing, and you will arrive soon enough at the destination.

The other way will take a little effort, time and money on your part, but in the long run, it will be cheaper. You can either pay now or later, but I can assure you that the later payment is more likely to be larger.

Now, it may not personally affect you, as you will be well on your way to that "deluxe apartment in the sky." (To keep the 70's illustrations going.) If you don't mind everybody knowing what you had, including the government and other attorneys getting their share before your heirs, then by all means, do nothing.

Legally they call the "do nothing" with estate planning, dying "intestate," meaning you died without a will. As a result, your estate will pass through the probate court system. Now, I wish I could cue some music that sounded like *dum da dum dum*, in a sort of menacing way, because I am not a fan of probate.

Let me state it clearly since I am in the financial pastoring business. I have three enemies: the adversary himself, inflation, and the probate court.

Now in all fairness, probate is a well-intentioned and often needed process whose purpose is to determine what is best and fair in contested circumstances. There are certainly times where some wishes are ambiguous, or an event or circumstance unforeseen.

In these cases the court appointed professionals perform a needed function, and the ones I have met have only worked in a caring manner.

What I fight against is the unnecessary utilization of the system because a person did not adequately prepare to avoid it. Either by inaction, or the failure to create the appropriate, legalized and recognized documents; or worse yet, creating the documents without completing the prescribed process.

This can happen either by failure to follow up as required, or due to outsiders who see a legal loophole and seek to gain benefits, never intended by the decedent.

So what happens in probate court?

Well, whatever does occur, occurs very slowly and expensively.

The court system in America is called upon to act on all sorts of issues, straining its ability to dispense justice promptly. This strain affects the probate court as well. Attorneys and judges have to line up their schedules. One attorney not being available can mean a 30-day delay. Then the other attorney is not ready, and there is another 30-day delay. Then the judge's dog has to have surgery, which results in a 60-day delay.

I am not very positive here, am I? Well, a quick internet search pulled up a consensus of the most favorable results, which if everyone agrees (a big IF), the probate process can take less than a year. And that was one of the most optimistic results. Another site said the average was 24 months. But the article noted if there is a will contest, it could take decades. Yes, decades.

One case I am currently working on has not even "officially" entered the probate system because there is a will contest surrounding it. (A will contest means someone does not like what the will said and has taken their request to the court to contest its validity. Some folks specifically choose a trust in addition to a will because it is not contestable in court.)

Did I mention the deceased passed over two and a half years ago?

Now can you imagine what has happened to the house without any care for two years? Or what was in the fridge? You can see my aversion to being "stuck" in probate; it is not just the cost. We have had two rounds of forced mediation so far. I just wish to know if the will was legal or not.

In the meantime, the attorneys got paid, so did the mediators. Besides, we got depositions from people in two states, again with attorneys present and multiple rounds of interrogatories, statements, and fact-finding all at a cost to the claimants and eventually to the estate. All of which could have been avoided with proper planning and up-to-date legal documents.

In addition to the expense and the delay of beneficiary payment, all of this process is public. Meaning it is all being recorded and made available for anyone who is interested in your business. It may just be me, but I am a private person and am not interested in the "looky Lous" poking their nose into my business.

Hopefully, I have convinced you that the "intestate" route is not your best option. Which means you will need to die "testate."

Meaning with a will, last testament and having a completed estate plan. With a properly created and funded estate plan, you can reduce, if not avoid, the entire process of probate.

Everyone will need a will.

However, a will does not avoid probate. It only identifies your wishes to the probate court and should be seen as an instruction sheet, which the court takes under advisement when it finally gets around to making its decisions. So, how does that help? Well, it is only one piece of your estate plan.

The rest of your estate plan will include proper documentation on non-probate transfer items. Some assets can pass through a beneficiary designation on the documents or have some other type of survivorship clause.

For instance, if you own real estate, you can place the name of a beneficiary who would inherit the property upon your passing, which is sometimes called a beneficiary deed or a transfer on death clause. This process must be done appropriately and registered, simply "telling" a person will not suffice. It is a simple but critical process.

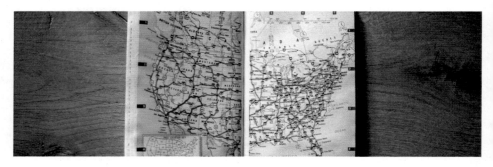

Based upon the state in which you live, lots of items can transfer via a similar means, but only if you do the proper, legally recognized paperwork. These are either referred to as "POD" Payable on Death or "TOD," Transfer on death. Retirement accounts can have these, IRA's, investment accounts, bank accounts, vehicles, and other motor vehicle titles. These are great ways that generally don't cost any money, but can save tons of time and money later.

For some people, there are reasons to take additional legal steps, such as creating a "Trust." A trust is a legal entity you and your spouse create in which you place all of your assets. By titling many of the above-listed assets into a trust, naming yourself a trustee, and having proper successor trustees, many of the above pitfalls are avoided.

A trust is not for everybody, but if you like to be doubly sure, have minor children, own a business, have a special needs family member, or have a complicated estate, it may well be worth the cost of consulting an attorney. We will discuss a trust later in a section devoted just to it, our purpose here is to raise the question. How do you want your estate to pass from you to your beneficiaries?

If you like things to move slowly, at a higher cost in a public manner, than doing nothing is the way to go. If you would rather avoid those types of things, then you need an estate plan titling non-probate transfer assets properly and should consider the possibility of a trust.

CHAPTER SIX

WHAT HAPPENS IF SOMETHING HAPPENS?

I was never a fan of the old cowboy shows. I was much more into Sci-Fi, but I can't say I was immune to their influence. Of course, the Lone Ranger and Tonto were the kings of the Cowboy show, sorry Roy Rogers. (you were great for sure though)

I preferred watching the Cisco Kid. By the way, the Cisco Kid was the first television show to be filmed in color, though most never saw the original run that way as only very few people had color TVs at that time.

I guess what attracted me to the show was the humor that Pancho brought; Tonto was always so serious. And every show would end with the same exchange. "Ohh Poncho," which was followed by "ohhh Cisco," followed by both of them laughing.

It was a great time.

There was always a shoot-out or two in all of the Old West TV shows, but there was never really any blood. It seems today we are required to see the blood and guts in as realistic a way as possible, but in those days, all you may have heard or seen was a "You got me," and watching the guy fall to the ground with no pain.

Many people seem to think that is the way they are going to go. One minute alive and well, the next minute, "you got me," or as Fred Sanford would say, "It's the big one Elizabeth, I'm coming home to see you." But for the majority of us, our passing may not come in one fell swoop. It may come on over days, months, or years.

The legal documents we have discussed so far: wills, trusts, and non-probate transfer mechanisms, only become active on your passing. They only work when you are dead. They do not provide any authority while you are alive. Whether you are completely incapacitated in a skilled nursing center never really getting out of bed, or if you become "forgetful," not able to make clear decisions, a will does absolutely nothing for you.

But there are legal means designed to provide for your care during these moments. These documents are called Powers of Attorney. We are going to discuss two of them—medical power of attorney and financial power of attorney. We are also going to present a third document called an Advance Medical Directive, sometimes called a living will.

A power of attorney is simply the legal right to act on behalf of another person. You don't have to hire or pay them like you do a typical attorney, but you are granting similar powers to them to make decisions that are binding and to take actions for you as if they are you.

While there are different categories of these powers such as: General, Durable, Springing, Limited (Special). We are going to focus more on their function.

The first is the medical power of attorney. This legal document grants the right for another person to make medical decisions on your behalf. Now each state has its particular language and often their specific materials, but they primarily work the same. This person makes medical decisions if you cannot make them on your own. Now, usually, one's spouse will have this right, but a legal document explicitly granting this right will move much more quickly when minutes matter.

A quick note about another document sometimes confusingly called a "living will" or more appropriately known as an Advance Medical Directive (AMD). It is a document you sign, before becoming incapacitated that provides proper written instructions informing the medical staff the kinds of things you want to be done, or not done in providing medical care. This helps guide your physicians and other caregivers around terminal or other end-of-life decisions.

Your wishes concerning "do not resuscitate" or life-sustaining measures, pain treatments, hydration, and nutrition. These are very difficult decisions to make for another person, particularly a spouse or child who is acting on your behalf. Many people want to remove that burden by having pre-decided these issues themselves via an AMD.

The medical power of attorney covers the types of decisions more related to treatments in recovery, or whether or not they have surgery to correct an issue rather than the end-of-life decisions.
Both the medical power of attorney and an AMD are needed; it is essential to have both to provide the gamete of care one might need.

The other power of attorney we mentioned is the financial power of attorney. It allows a person to make financial and other business-related decisions on your behalf. The document will typically be limited, granting only the capabilities specifically outlined in the legal document.

Such ability to limit, means the document and the rights granted can be as specific or general as you desire. They can either be very long documents or very brief. You can limit "who" and "what" can be done on your behalf.

Maybe you have a son who is a part of the family business in which you still make decisions. You may want to grant him the authority to act on your behalf in that business. But you want your daughter to handle your personal banking account.

You might need two documents whose power do not overlap with one another as opposed to one trying to grant powers to each.

Most of the time, though, you may want to leave as a general authority as possible. This kind of document is called a general power of attorney. It gives an extensive amount of authority and can be more beneficial in certain instances.

But even these documents can be limited, so again it will be best to consult legal counsel on what is best in your particular circumstance.

The other kind is a springing power of attorney, meaning something has to happen before it "springs" into effect. The most common is a requirement that a physician or two physicians must certify a person being medically incapacitated before the authority is transferred to the previously identified power of attorney.

There are pros and cons to each of these. For my 85-year-old father, we have a durable power of attorney, because we never know what might happen that would require us to take action. In other cases, the emotional need for another required step is healthy; a springing one may work better. Either way, these documents are vital for almost every estate plan.

Many attorneys will provide a basic estate planning kit that provides a Will, Advance Medical Directives, and some Medical and Financial Powers of Attorney. The basic estate planning package is usually in the range of hundreds of dollars. If one wanted to add a trust to the estate planning package, then you will be talking in the thousands of dollars. (Pay me now or pay me later).

But the second and equally important action will be required no matter the plan or package, determining who you trust to act on your behalf for not only when you are alive, but after you pass.

CHAPTER SEVEN

WHO DO YOU TRUST?

For the 18th year in a row, nurses were the most highly ranked profession in Gallup's annual survey of most honest and trustworthy professions, with 85% rating them either "high" or "very high." Clergy, my official designation, finished about midway with 45% in the high or very high category. Right in between chiropractors and journalists. Ouch. We did outpace Stockbrokers, Advertising practitioners, Insurance salespeople, Senators just ahead of Members of Congress, and at the very bottom of the list Car salespeople who garnered a 12% rating.

Now, of course, we know people in each of those professions who are honest professionals, and we know some people who are not so much. As my brother-in-law often says, half of all people are below average. (He stares rather intently at me, pausing as if he wants me to understand something profound, maybe even something about myself.)

So, we are not talking about any particular person. It is ok if you are a car salesman, but one has to recognize the general view of the profession. Honest car salespeople are usually highly sought after because of the perception of there being so few of them.

However, I am not sure about finding a trustworthy member of Congress. But, trust is a precious commodity in this world where it is so often broken.

Trust is developed over time by demonstrating consistent and appropriate behavior. So your task is to determine the people you trust to oversee the transition of your estate. You may choose the same person for each of the three categories we are going to discuss, or you may have reason to select the person more particularly suited to the task at hand.

Just because a person is related to you does not mean they are qualified. Just because you have known someone for a long time, and known them well, may not mean you have a pretty good handle on how they are going to behave after you are gone. Pretty much like they acted when you were around, but probably worse. It actually might be more difficult to select a family member.

Before we begin selecting people, let us take a look at the kinds of task which will be needed to be assigned. Then we can begin the process of selection of these pivotal people in our planning process.

Let's first start with powers of attorney. You will need to select someone to make your medical decisions and become your medical power of attorney. This is a significant decision, and its not the time to be worried about hurting someone's feelings. It must be a person who cares deeply for you, but appropriately. Meaning you don't want to leave the responsibility to someone who never really liked you and can benefit from your passing.

Lest they take a more pragmatic approach and too quickly turn off machines, withhold viable treatments and takes some form of action or inaction that leads to their inheriting their share of the estate prematurely.

But it also should be someone tough enough to make the right call. One must consider the burden resting on the individual and their emotional constitution. It should not fall to the shoulders of a person who could never handle the thought of being the one who decided on your treatment plan that did not work.

If you have a sensitive child, the one who stops to help turtles along the side of the road, making the tough emotional call, might not serve them well. They may have some other roles to play, but if they "could never live with themselves," knowing they withheld a life-sustaining treatment don't ask them to play this role.

Another caution, sometimes a person will decide to let the children collectively decide. This idea sounds nice so that they all can share the burden of decision making, but in practice, it hardly ever works. What if one child opts for one process, the other child believes the other is better? You either have a stalemate or the third child casting a tie-breaking vote, further alienating the dissenter. No, it is usually better to name one person, the decision-maker.

But always think to include a successor or a secondary decision-maker just in case the person is not available due to travel or their circumstances. Because people do die, having a secondary POA lessens the likelihood of not having a person to serve. You may also want to consider geography in the mix. While a person can decide on the phone or electronic communication concerning one's care, there is something about being there that cannot be replaced. Also, choosing one who has a more comprehensive knowledge of ongoing medical conditions and their most recent state of well-being can prove to be helpful.

Similar concerns should be explored for the financial power of attorney decisions as well. A person who has a good business sense, can handle money well, and has no personal interest in the financial assets under their care are worthy of consideration.

Familiarity with the overall economic picture of the person and at least a basic understanding of financial matters is helpful.

Now when it comes to after your passing, you will need to name a Personal Representative. Sometimes this is called an Executor. You identify this person in your Will. They will have the responsibility of seeing to all of your intentions are carried out under state law.

The role will take some time and effort on their part and can include a variety of duties. Items like cleaning up the house after a passing, liquidating the property, listing the home for sale, transfer money to beneficiaries, paying final expenses, working with the courts, etc.

Because of the effort, the law allows for the taking of a fee for their services. Sometimes family members decline, but they are eligible to take them.

Again, consider listing a secondary or successor personal representative, should something happen to the person you named first, is critical.

One never knows what might happen over time. The naming of additional people is even more critical if you were to elect to create a trust. A trustee can begin to perform their function before a person passes away. A person can resign from being their trustee and allow their successor trustee to replace them.

This exchange can be especially helpful for the person whose mental capacity begins to decline and needs protection from poor decision making or scam artists. It is also useful for the one who simply does not want to deal with the complexity of bill paying, tax compliance, or other issues.

Naming more than one trustee can be done.

Two children may equally share the role as a co-trustee, but this arrangement can also cause problems as the trust language may require both or just one acting, which could lead to all kinds of issues should the two not act together or one working in a rogue manner.

Naming a successor trustee for the reasons listed above is a prudent move. And as in the case of a personal rep, a trustee can take fees from the estate.

We have been thinking in terms of these roles as individuals, but did you also realize you could name a corporation as a power of attorney, personal representative, or trustee? There are several benefits.

The first is that a corporation does not usually die, individuals always will. By naming a person, it is only a matter of time before they pass away, and you run the risk of not having someone to serve.

I know of one situation where three single ladies, with no children, had committed to taking care of each other.

For years this arrangement worked as they helped each other make doctor appointments, buy groceries, and share decision making.

It worked well until only one of the three remained. She needed a new plan, which included a corporation.

I serve as the President of an organization that began way back in 1946. While not everyone born the same year has passed away, it is only a matter of time.

All of the principal players in our founding are no longer alive, but the corporation, and our sacred responsibilities continue.

People of every decade have named the Missouri Baptist Foundation as their representative. I do not know many of them, but I serve them through our corporate and ministry relationship.

One day another staff will come along and help those with whom we forged a relationship, all without interruption of service.

I recently began serving as a personal representative for a person I never met. They completed their will back in the 1980s when I was still in high school. They never met me, but they met someone from the Foundation and placed their trust in our organization. By doing so, they and their estate are receiving the same care and concern through me.

We call this serving in a fiduciary capacity. (We are required by law to act on behalf of the client's interest and according to their instruction.)

The other main benefit, while there are many, is that we "live in the world of estate settlement." Most people can follow the steps as they are not "rocket science," but for the person who has never "settled an estate," it can be unsettling. Mainly because of the inherently emotional nature of working through their loved one's possessions.

More people are finding value in those tasks being delegated elsewhere.

Family members often have to take time away from their work, while this is part of our corporations work. They may have to incur the expense and time of being far away from their home to complete these tasks when we can do so in fulfillment of our profession.

My goal is not to persuade you to name a corporation rather than an individual, only to consider the options.

Please also know other organizations can serve as well. Such as banks, for instance, or trust companies. MBF can only help those who have a benevolent or philanthropic plan, (the reason for our book is an invitation to make a substantial investment in God's Kingdom), but there are a growing number of other options for those who only want to provide for family.

I would at least encourage you to name a corporation at least as a secondary personal representative, trustee, or attorney, just in case.

Still, for many people who either don't have someone to name, anyone they trust or that don't want their loved ones to be bothered, a corporation could be a wise decision.

So, we have almost completed our journey.

WHAT DO YOU HAVE?
WHERE DO YOU WANT IT TO GO?
HOW DO YOU WANT IT TO GET THERE?
WHAT HAPPENS IF SOMETHING HAPPENS?
WHO DO YOU TRUST TO GET IT THERE?

This discussion leaves us with one final question, and it may be the most important one.

WHAT IF YOU COULD DO MORE?

CHAPTER EIGHT

WHAT IF YOU COULD DO MORE?

I had only been on the job for a couple of weeks. I had left a magnificent church where I was blessed to be called pastor, to a new role serving our denomination.

It was my task on this particular day to attend a scholarship banquet in which the Foundation, for which I worked, managed several scholarships. It would be my privilege to meet and present to a few of the winners.

I introduced myself and tried to explain the role of the Foundation to the students, who only partially understood the 'dog and pony show' nature of the luncheon. It was here where I met Lexa. She was a first-generation college student who did grasp the value of our time together.

I told her congratulations on winning the Mary Gibbs scholarship, which is when it hit me.

I did not know who Mary Gibbs' was. I was nervous, I felt like I should have known who she was and I sure hoped she was ok with me giving her money away.

I continued with the small talk for the next hour around the table of the other scholarship winners, but I could not get it out of my head. Who was Mary Gibbs?

The next day I returned to the office to begin my search for Ms. Gibbs. It was not long before the computer produced the results. Sure enough, Mary Gibbs entrusted some money to the Missouri Baptist Foundation to send kids to college. How noble I thought, what a great way to leave a legacy, to invest in the next generation.

But, what I was about to read was going to change my whole view of the kind of impact one person could make.

You see, Mary Gibbs died in 1921. Yes, you read that correctly 94 years after her passing, Ms. Gibbs was still helping send kids to college. I have since handed the scholarship out two more times, and each time it was a larger check than the year before.

Like Randy Alcorn said in his book <u>The Treasure Principle</u>, Ms. Gibbs has done more from Heaven financially for the Gospel than she ever did while on earth. And you can, too, if you make a plan.

For most of us, we need our stuff while we are here on earth. I need my salary, my car, and my cat needs the cat food I have the privilege of purchasing for her.

But, when I die, I don't need any of those things. Remember what I said earlier; they don't take the US dollar in Heaven, or Hell.

Now, before you get too far ahead of me, I am not suggesting leaving everything to a Gospel advancing ministry and bypassing your children. (I am hoping my father leaves me something in his Will) But you could leave something.

The something could be the largest single gift you ever give.

When we talk with people who are planning their estates, we like them to consider one of three options.

I mentioned them earlier: **GIVING 10%, EQUAL HEIRS, OR GIVE IT TWICE**

GIVING 10%

The first option is the 'give a tithe' concept.

Of course, you know the word "tithe" means tenth taken, from the old English. It comes from an Old Testament concept. I am not here to debate whether the tithe is still a New Testament concept or not. Many other more scholarly sorts than I have done so.

We point out that for some people, they may wish to leave a specific portion or percentage of their estate to their local church or other ministries they had or always wanted to support and ten percent seems to be a good place to start.

Some people have also chosen to leave a specific amount. Say the first $10,000 or the first $100,000.

These are not bad ideas either, but remember, over time, due to inflation, those amounts will not maintain the same buying power.

We have some beneficiaries who receive $10 annually from a trust fund. Back when it was created in Mary Gibbs day $10 was a lot of money; now, the youth ministry won't even be able to buy a pizza for the retreat.

Again, I am not here to propose any particular amount or percentage; it is your decision as to what you want to do with the Lord entrusted.

But including at least 10% of your estate going to ministries, we believe it is an excellent place to start.

EQUAL HEIRS

Another way of leaving a part of your estate is through what we call 'Equal Heirs'.

The idea here is for you to consider all of your philanthropic giving as one of your children. Here you would include your giving to your church, mission projects, the children's home, your local university, whatever you have been giving to support and want to continue to help.

You put them in one "bucket" if you will. Then include all of those endeavors as an additional child.

Let's say you have two children, under the equal heirs plan you would divide your estate by three instead of two. If you had three children, then each of them would get 25% of your estate, and your charities would also get a total of 25%.

Of course, you will need to subdivide further how much each charity would receive from the share, but at least both children and ministry will gain something.

Most children, especially those who know of their parents' generosity, are quite comfortable with either of the above arrangements.

However, it is up to the one who is creating the estate plan to decide as it is their resources.

Children should never presume that what their parents earned is theirs.

GIVE IT TWICE

There is a third and creative way, through which can sometimes create a ruffling of feathers effect, though it might be entirely appropriate given the circumstances.

We call this plan the 'Give it Twice.'

This will require a shift in thinking. Before entering the ministry of estate planning, and I do see it as a ministry as I help people be generous and demonstrate their faith and love of Jesus, I just assumed that once a person dies their assets must be immediately distributed.

However, that is not the case; first off, the probate process can take many months, and it can take time to liquidate certain assets.

With proper planning, the estate can continue indefinitely, creating income and allowing for annual distributions without disturbing the initial amount of the estate.

While the very wealthy have always known of such tools, even the middle class with just a little planning can make a sizable and lasting difference in the life of a ministry.

THE SOUL

By far the greater impact is on the individual soul, which is why you are still reading.

You are like my friends the Day's. They are a middle class family who has a heart for ministry. They love their church, they actively support their local children's home, but are have never been able to give much. They live simple lives, under their financial means as their heart is set on the next Kingdom.

When I first met them, they too did not think they had much to give, but as we explored the Give it Twice option, their hearts began to catch fire. We ran a simple excel spread sheet calculating the impact of their middle class estate could have on ministry over time.

They were amazed and said, we have always wanted to give hundreds of thousands of dollars away, but we never had it. Now we will, even if it will be over the decades after our passing.

In their eyes I saw the joy I want you to experience. They experienced the thrill of knowing that they will be giving to Jesus exponentially more than what they ever thought they could give. It won't be during their lifetime. It won't be everything they have as they are leaving support for their son and their "special" grandson, but it will amount to potentially a half a million dollars.

They are thrilled.

Let me show you how the math works. In our scenario, suppose when you pass away, you have an estate valued at $600,000. This is not an unusually high amount if you have a paid-for house, a modest saving account, and a couple of retirement accounts.

At your passing you could split the estate between your two children leaving each $300,000 or $270,000 if you were to tithe on your estate first. If you were to include your charitable giving as a third child, then each would receive $200,000.

But, if you decided to distribute your estate over time, you could actually double the amount.

Suppose you were to create a trust and instruct your trustee to invest your full estate and make only an annual distribution to your two children.

You could set a certain percentage or a specific amount. For this example, let use a 10% distribution rate for 12 years. The invested funds would grow at a lower rate, let's say 5%.

At the end of the 12 years, anything left in the account would go to your favorite ministry. This allows, the kids to get their money first, and the ministry later.

Do you want to guess how much money the children would have received over those twelve years and how much the ministry would receive at the end?

Well, I won't bore you with the mathematical equation, but I think you will be surprised.

The children will have received in total $564,476.71 between the two of them!

Just short of the $600,000 they would have split initially; they would be even closer in year 13 if the time frame was extended.

Beginning in year 14, they will start receiving more than the original total.

But the impact on ministry is even more incredible. Even with all of those annual distributions, there is still over $340,000 left to give to the ministry.

While not quite doubling the money, the $600,000 has grown to over $900,000. Not a bad benefit for both the family and the charity.

All this gained by just taking a longer view of estate planning.

Of course, there are no guarantees on the actual gains as markets fluctuate. There may also be some drop in value due to inflation over the twelve years, but I think the point cannot be lost.

EVERYONE HAS GAINED

Your estate can be invested over time, doing more of what you intended. You enjoy the thrill of knowing you are giving significantly to the work of God's Kingdom, your children receive their inheritance and the ministry you selected, continues to Advance the Gospel for years to come.

Your estate can also create an endowment that lasts into perpetuity, a fancy word for forever. Instead the ministry receiving the total amount in an outright distribution at the end of year twelve, the ministry begins receiving the annual distribution previously given to the children while the principal (what remained of the gift) continues to be invested.

This is how Mrs. Gibbs money continues to produce ministry results a hundred years later.

Again, you will need to consult your estate planning attorney and tax accountant for the specifics; I just want you to be aware of the possibilities.

And the great news is you can do something like Ms. Gibbs and maybe even watch from Heaven for a century or beyond. You will see how the dollars you left on earth are helping people hear the Gospel and make Heaven their eternal home as well.

CONCLUSION

KNOWING IS HALF OF THE BATTLE

So now you have it.

The basics of building your estate plan.

Now what?

Well, now comes the hard part. Just as GI Joe of the 1980s used to say,

"NOW YOU KNOW AND KNOWING IS HALF THE BATTLE."

What he failed to mention is knowing was the easy half. Learning is pretty easy; it is the doing part that gets most of us.

In James chapter one, we are warned not to be hearers only, but doers.

So what are you to do?

Well, you follow the steps answering each of the six questions. If you forgot what they are, then consult the <u>end of the book</u> where you will find the questions, along with a helpful recap of the topics covered and items to consider.

The next thing you may want to do is download our My Financial Pastor planning guide. ⬇

In it, you will find a helpful notebook in which you can start writing down your information. You can utilize a fillable PDF version or download a printable copy.

After that, you may want to reach out to us here at <u>myfinanicalpastor.com</u> or with our sister ministry <u>mbfn.org</u> and have a complementary and confidential visit. Both organizations do one-on-one consulting for no fee either via the phone, online or in-person allowing you an interactive format to talk out your plan.

Our experts have helped many clients, and you can surely benefit from their expertise and wisdom. There is no obligation, and never will you feel pressure from us to do anything in particular; well, other than just doing something.

Then you are ready to meet with an attorney to draw up the documents. We recommend reaching out to an attorney who specializes in estate planning.

While any attorney can do a will, not every one of them should. We suggest you look for an estate planning attorney. It would not be a bad idea to include your financial planner or your tax accountant as well. Building a highly qualified team can lead to greater success long-term.

We have also accompanied individuals to their first meeting with their legal professionals upon request.

We can review your completed documents to sort of serve as a translator of legalese and English if you would like. We will do just about anything to make sure you do something.

For those of you who are more likely to do it yourself, there are other approaches as well.

Medical directives are rather easy to find online; make sure you follow th directions correctly and have them on file at numerous places, including your local physician's office and medical facility.

The other documents like POA's, and Wills are available online in an inexpensive format, remember you get for what you pay.

Legalzoom, Freewill and Mama Bear, are all current options.

The Missouri Bar also provides some helpful information on their website You don't have to utilize legal counsel to accomplish most of the steps, but we highly recommend it. Especially for those of you who want to think outside of the box; who are not content to be among the majority.

We end our journey, the same place we began, with an invitation.

> *Yes, you should have an estate plan to protect and care for your loved ones.*

> *Yes, you want to make sure you maximize your resources for your beneficiary's in the most efficient means possible.*

But more than that, don't you want to "feel" the pleasure of God by knowing that you are leaving a portion of your earthly possessions to hel others find a heavenly home?

Sincerely,

Neil Franks

Dr. Neil Franks CEP®
Your Financial Pastor

index

1 https://www.caring.com/caregivers/estate-planning/wills-survey

2 All images are royalty free images curtosy of the users of unsplash.com

3 Source http://www.ugapress.org/

ESTATE PLANNING QUESTIONNAIRE

PREPARING YOU
TO PREPARE

Dr. Neil Franks
Missouri Baptist Foundation

table of contents

Personal Information

FULL NAME

SPOUSE NAME

PHONE

PHONE

EMAIL

EMAIL

BIRTH DATE

BIRTH DATE

ADDRESS

DO YOU HAVE A PRE- OR POST-NUPTIAL AGREEMENT? YES ☐ NO ☐

PRINT YOUR NAMES EXACTLY HOW YOU SIGN THEM.
(INDICATE IF YOU USE YOUR MIDDLE INITIAL).

Family Information

FULL NAME	BIRTH DATE	ADDRESS (CITY & STATE)	CHILDREN

FULL NAME	BIRTH DATE	ADDRESS (CITY & STATE)	CHILDREN

FULL NAME	BIRTH DATE	ADDRESS (CITY & STATE)	CHILDREN

FULL NAME	BIRTH DATE	ADDRESS (CITY & STATE)	CHILDREN

FULL NAME	BIRTH DATE	ADDRESS (CITY & STATE)	CHILDREN

Health Information

PLEASE IDENTIFY YOUR PRIMARY CARE PHYSICIAN AND LIST
SERIOUS MEDICAL CONDITIONS, IF ANY.

YOU	SPOUSE

Current Documents

HAVE YOU MADE YOUR FUNERAL OR BURIAL ARRANGEMENTS?
YOU: YES ☐ NO ☐ SPOUSE: YES ☐ NO ☐

DO YOU OR YOUR SPOUSE WANT TO DONATE YOUR ORGANS?
YOU: YES ☐ NO ☐ SPOUSE: YES ☐ NO ☐

DO YOU OR YOUR SPOUSE WANT YOUR AGENT IN A DURABLE POWER
OF ATTORNEY TO BE ABLE TO REQUEST AN AUTOPSY?
YOU: YES ☐ NO ☐ SPOUSE: YES ☐ NO ☐

EITHER OF YOU A VETERAN? YES ☐ NO ☐

DO YOU OR YOUR SPOUSE HAVE LONG TERM CARE INSURANCE?
YOU: YES ☐ NO ☐ SPOUSE: YES ☐ NO ☐

Assets/Debits

SAVINGS BOND SERIES	ISSUE DATE	FACE VALUE	OWNER
TOTAL			

BANK ACCOUNTS	BANK NAME	BALANCE	OWNER
TOTAL			

Assets/Debits

MUTUAL FUNDS/STOCKS/BONDS	COMPANY OR BROKERAGE	FACE VALUE	OWNER
TOTAL			

RETIREMENT ACCOUNTS	COMPANY OR BROKERAGE	VALUE	OWNER & BENEFICIARIES
TOTAL			

LIFE INSURANCE COMPANY	FACE VALUE	CASH VALUE	NAMES OF INSURED, OWNER, BENEFICIARY
TOTAL FACE VALUE			

Debts

PROMISSORY NOTES, ACCOUNTS RECEIVABLE & OTHER FUNDS OWED TO YOU OR YOUR SPOUSE. EXPLAIN NATURE OF DEBT (FOR EXAMPLE, PERSONAL LOAN OR PROMISSORY NOTE SECURED BY DEED OF TRUST)	AMOUNT OWED TO YOU &/OR YOUR SPOUSE	BORROWER'S NAME(S)
TOTAL DEBT VALUE		

AS TO ANY MONEY OWED TO YOU, DO YOU WANT AN OFFSET AFTER YOU DIE AGAINST DISTRIBUTIONS TO YOUR FAMILY MEMBERS WHO OWE YOU MONEY? YES ☐ NO ☐

ENTER CREDITOR AND TYPE (E.G., MORTGAGE ON HOME, VEHICLE LOAN, CREDIT CARD, PERSONAL LOAN, CO-SIGNING FOR FAMILY MEMBER)	AMOUNT OWED	BORROWER'S NAME(S)
TOTAL DEBT OWED		

Income

TYPE	YOURSELF	SPOUSE
TOTAL		

DO YOU OR YOUR SPOUSE HAVE A SAFE DEPOSIT BOX? IF YES, IDENTIFY LOCATION(S) & CONTENTS:

Fiduciaries

I.E., WHO WILL MAKE DECISIONS OR MANAGE YOUR ESTATE WHEN YOU CANNOT?

WHEN WE PREPARE DOCUMENTS, A FIDUCIARY IS THE PERSON WHOM YOU ENTRUST TO TAKE CARE OF YOU WHEN YOU ARE:
INCAPACITATED OR YOUR ASSETS OR IF YOU ARE DISABLED OR DECEASED.

THESE FIDUCIARIES MIGHT BE AN INSTITUTIONAL TRUSTEE:
A BANK TRUST DEPARTMENT, AN INDIVIDUAL, SUCH AS AN ADULT CHILD OR A SIBLING.

THEY WILL HAVE VERY IMPORTANT
SPECIFIC DUTIES AND RESPONSIBILITIES AS SET OUT IN STATE LAW FOR EACH TYPE OF DOCUMENT.

PLEASE CHOOSE QUALIFIED PERSONS WHOM YOU TRUST TO SERVE AS FIDUCIARIES FOR EACH OF THE DOCUMENTS BELOW:

WHO WILL FOLLOW YOUR INSTRUCTIONS, PREFERENCES, AND WISHES. FOR EXAMPLE, SOMEONE WHO WORKS IN A BANK OR IS AN ACCOUNTANT MIGHT BE GOOD TO ASSIST YOU WITH MANAGING YOUR FINANCES AND YOUR PROPERTY WHILE SOMEONE WHO IS WORKING IN THE HEALTHCARE FIELD MIGHT BE GOOD TO SERVE AS YOUR AGENT UNDER YOUR DURABLE POWER OF ATTORNEY FOR HEALTHCARE.

PLEASE INDICATE YOUR CHOICES BELOW, IN ORDER OF PREFERENCE, AND BE PREPARED TO DISCUSS YOUR CHOICES WITH THE LAWYER.

Trust Information

FULL NAME

RELATION

FULL NAME

RELATION

FULL NAME

RELATION

PERSONAL REPRESENTIVES

FULL NAME

RELATION

FULL NAME

RELATION

FULL NAME

RELATION

NAME OF TRUST: WHAT WOULD YOU WANT TO NAME IT?
(EXAMPLE: "SMITH TRUST" OR "SMITH FAMILY TRUST")

AGENTS UNDER FINANCIAL POA

FULL NAME	RELATION
FULL NAME	RELATION
FULL NAME	RELATION

AGENTS UNDER HEALTHCARE POA

NAME, ADDRESS, PHONE #	NAME, ADDRESS, PHONE #

HIPAA

"HIPAA" STANDS FOR "HEALTH INSURANCE PORTABILITY AND ACCOUNTABILITY ACT,"

A LAW REQUIRING CERTAIN SAFEGUARDS TO PROTECT CONFIDENTIAL MEDICAL INFORMATION. IF YOU WANT MEMBERS OF YOUR FAMILY, FRIENDS, TRUSTEES, AND OTHERS TO FIND OUT ABOUT HOW YOU ARE DOING IN THE HOSPITAL OR NURSING HOME, THEN YOU NEED TO AUTHORIZE THE HOSPITAL, NURSING HOME, AND STAFF TO RELEASE INFORMATION TO THEM.

IF YOU WANT THE PHYSICIAN, NURSE, COUNSELOR, OR OTHER HEALTHCARE PROVIDER TO DISCUSS YOUR MEDICAL STATUS WITH SOMEONE ELSE, YOU NEED TO AUTHORIZE THAT PERSON TO BE ABLE TO TALK TO YOUR HEALTHCARE PROVIDER.

PLEASE INDICATE BELOW THE PERSONS WHO SHOULD BE AUTHORIZED TO RECEIVE MEDICAL INFORMATION FROM YOUR HEALTHCARE PROVIDERS ABOUT STATUS, DIAGNOSIS, AND PROGNOSIS:

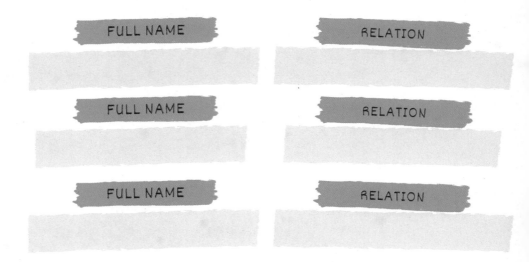

MISCELLANEOUS

IT IS IMPORTANT THAT YOU TELL THE LAWYER ABOUT ANY SPECIAL NEEDS OR CONDITIONS INVOLVING YOUR CHILDREN OR OTHER HEIRS. DOES YOUR LAWYER NEED TO KNOW ANY SPECIAL INFORMATION ABOUT ANY PERSONS TO RECEIVE YOUR PROPERTY, OR NOT RECEIVE IT, AFTER YOU DIE?

FOR EXAMPLE, ARE YOU ESTRANGED FROM ANY OF YOUR CHILDREN IS THERE ANY PERSON WHO HAS SPECIAL NEEDS OR OTHER CONSIDERATIONS SUCH AS A SPOUSE DIAGNOSED WITH ALZHEIMER'S, A CHILD WHO IS DEVELOPMENTALLY DISABLED, CHILD WHO HAS MARITAL PROBLEMS, A CHILD WITH MENTAL ILLNESS, A CHILD WITH HEALTH PROBLEMS, OR A CHILD WHO HAS FILED FOR BANKRUPTCY? ARE THERE CHILDREN FROM PREVIOUS MARRIAGES, ADOPTED CHILDREN, A BLENDED FAMILY, A CHILD WHO PREDECEASED PARENTS, A CHILD WHO CANNOT MANAGE MONEY, OR A CHILD BORN OUTSIDE OF MARRIAGE?

IF YES AS TO ANY SPECIAL INFORMATION, PLEASE EXPLAIN:

DISTRIBUTION INSTRUCTIONS

HOW AND TO WHOM DO YOU WANT YOUR PROPERTY TO BE DISTRIBUTED UPON YOUR DEATH? DO YOU WANT TO GIVE SOMETHING TO A CHARITY?

FOR EXAMPLE, "$1,000.00 (OR 5% OF TOTAL) TO BE DISTRIBUTED TO GRANDCHILDREN, REMAINDER TO CHILDREN;" OR "$1,000.00 (OR 5% OF TOTAL) TO "MY CHURCH" OF "CITY", "STATE", THEN REMAINDER DIVIDED EQUALLY AMONG MY CHILDREN"

Made in the USA
Monee, IL
21 February 2022